THE L

WRONG

SHUI

Rohan Candappa

Andrews McMeel
Publishing

Kansas City

First publication by Ebury Press in Great Britain 1999

The Little Book of Wrong Shui copyright © 2000 by
Rohan Candappa. All rights reserved. Printed in the United
States of America. No part of this book may be used or
reproduced in any manner whatsoever without written
permission except in the case of reprints in the context of
reviews. For information, write Andrews McMeel Publishing,
an Andrews McMeel Universal company,
4520 Main Street, Kansas City, Missouri 64111.

00 01 02 03 04 BIN 10 9 8 7 6 5 4

ISBN: 0-7407-0475-3

Library of Congress Catalog Card Number: 99-67128

ABOUT THE AUTHOR

This is the bit that blathers on about what an interesting and talented person the author is. Well, frankly, he's not. I know him quite well and he's a fraud. His wife is far nicer and more talented, his cats are better company and his "books," *The Little Book of Stress* and *The Stocking Filler*, aren't exactly an oeuvre. My advice is that you should avoid him. But why should you listen to me? I only write author blurbs. What I'm really working on is a novel. . . . Hey! Come back!

FOR JAN

INTRODUCTION

Many people ask me about Wrong Shui. And the first question they ask is always the same. And I always reply with the same answer. I say, "Rong Shoe Ee— that's how you pronounce it." Then they ask me whether it works. I reply with the explanation I first heard from the lips of The Master all those many years ago. I say, "Yes." This book is but a brief introduction to Wrong Shui. It is a signpost along the path. And the path is long. Wrong Shui changed my life. Study well and it will change your life too.

THE LONGEST JOURNEY STARTS WITH A SINGLE STEP

(BEING A BRIEF INTRODUCTION TO THE JOURNEY OF MASTER EU PLON KA AND THE GENESIS OF WRONG SHUI)

Master Eu Plon Ka came from a wealthy family in the ancient city of Pushtu. His family had made their fortune from the lucrative slow loris trade. He grew up a privileged child waited on hand, foot, and mouth. Every morning he would be dressed and fed by doting servants. When he finally became a man by strangling a yew tree at the age of seventeen, he inherited the business and the luxury went on unabated until one fateful day.

On the day of the annual beak auctions, his shoe servant made an error that would change everything. The servant put two unmatching shoes next to each other and when Master Eu slipped them on it was clear that one was much higher than the other.

But Eu was a powerful man and no one dared point out the faux pas as he strode lopsidedly toward the auction room.

In the auction room a terrible thing happened. The uneven shoes totally unbalanced Master Eu's view and judgment. He staked his family's entire fortune on a dubious consignment of beaks—a consignment that when taken out into the cold winter sun, immediately curdled.

Master Eu was ruined. He'd lost everything.

As he despondently trudged home,
a small boy started laughing at his
lopsided gait. Master Eu sat by the
roadside and contemplated his
unmatching shoes.

And it was then that he was granted
the revelation that the course of his
whole life had turned upon the
unhappy accident of the wrong object,
in the wrong place, at the wrong time.

In this case a wrong shoe.

*Master Eu never removed those shoes.
Instead he set off on a deeply
contemplative, obliquely angled
odyssey around the world developing
his unique philosophy.*

The philosophy of Wrong Shui.

I met Master Eu Plon Ka in a
retail outlet just outside Warrington.
He was an old man. A very old man.
But a very wise one.

He took me under his wing and let me
walk by his side. In the months that
followed he schooled me in the
teachings of Wrong Shui.

And it is these teachings I humbly
share with you. I hope you will find

them as useful, insightful, and profound as I have.

The last time I saw Master Eu he was tottering off toward the setting sun reading a copy of Bella.

He was eating a kipper.

I miss him.

Rohan Candappa, Winter, London

NICE TO SEE YOU

Attract visitors to your home by
placing stereo, video, and computer
equipment where they can be
seen from the road.

CONVERSATION PIECE

To encourage conversation
always have one fewer chair
than there are guests at a
dinner party.

Sweet and Sour

Storing sugar in the salt cellar
and salt in the sugar bowl will help
to discourage complacency in
many ways.

POINTY PLANTS

Plants with pointy leaves
are bad for you.

So are friends with pointy
faces. Avoid both.

DEFEND YOUR
SACRED SPACES

The space directly in front of your
house is sacred. It is here that you
should practice Wrong Shui's
sister art of Ka Pa King.

On no account let anyone occupy
this sacred space.

USE YOUR LOAF

If your toast always lands
butter-side down, plan ahead.

Butter the other side instead.

WATER AND WEALTH

If you own a chain of fast-food
restaurants, then an abundance of ice,
judiciously positioned in cups
of soft drink, will do wonders
for your wealth sector.

TOILET TRAINING

Toilets are notoriously bad
Wrong Shui. If you must have
one inside the house refrain from
using it. Instead pop next door
and use your neighbor's.

Scaring Off Evil Spirits

In ancient times wind chimes
were used to scare off evil spirits.
In modern times car alarms serve
much the same purpose. Rig your car
alarm to go off at regular intervals
throughout the night. Then you
will be able to sleep peacefully,
knowing you are safe.

RECAPTURING THE SPARK

Nylon sheets, positioned on the bed,
will help to regenerate electricity
in a floundering marriage.

DOORS

Try to ensure that your front
door is at the edge of your home.
Internal front doors are bad
Wrong Shui.

More Doors

Always have a Doors CD
in your home.

Preferably *Strange Days*.

A BRIGHT IDEA

If parts of your home are prone to
darkness, a light, carefully located,
will solve the problem.

DISH IT OUT

If your neighbor has a satellite
dish pointing in your direction, this
focuses harmful "secret arrows"
on to your home.

Wait till night,
then take the dish down.

THE WRONG SHUI
OF SMALL OFFICES

If you work in a small, cramped,
cluttered office, then your boss
doesn't like you and you really
should get another job.

TOILET TRAINING, ADVANCED

Keep the seat down on the toilet at all times.

Even when you're using it.

PULL YOURSELF TOGETHER

Curtains should never be drawn.

It is much better if they
are lightly sketched.

SEE RED

In Wrong Shui red is an
extremely lucky color. That is
why it is far more auspicious to
wait until any utility bill turns
red before paying it.

THE UPS AND DOWNS
OF STAIRS

Stairs going up are good
Wrong Shui.

In your home only have
stairs going up.

MIND THE GAP

Removing the occasional floorboard
from your home will help
generate in you, and in those who visit
you, a heightened sense of
awareness of your surroundings.

A LESSON FROM THE MASTER

It had been raining all day. Dallas had just been knocked out of the Super Bowl play-offs. And a warm front was fast approaching from the coast. Master Eu was ensconced in a chili cheese dog while contemplatively sipping from a translucent Tupperware beaker of Dr. Pepper. My mind raced back to our first meeting all those months ago in line D at the Service Merchandise pick-up counter. He was waiting for a Barbie typewriter and I was waiting for an adjustable ironing-board cover (red). Something about his demeanor drew me to him. I'd never seen a sandwich held at such a jaunty yet knowing angle before. I tried to engage him in pleasantries, but he ignored me. I noticed that a drop of chili sauce had dripped onto my shoe. Little did I know that this chance encounter would alter my life for ever. On his way out he pulled me to one side and whispered the words that changed everything.

"If a ship is sinking," he said, "then maybe the rats have a point."

How true.

GO WITH THE FLOW

Flowing water is good Wrong Shui.
So when winter approaches
remove a couple of tiles or shingles
from the roof of your home.

DON'T BE BYPASSED

If a road runs outside your front
door, this means you will be
bypassed in life. Dig up the road at the
earliest possible opportunity.

WHEN THE LIGHT GOES OUT

Defective light bulbs will only have
blown for a reason. Usually the reason
is connected with your career or
matters of personal hygiene. It is bad
Wrong Shui to replace the bulb until
you have resolved the matter.

POCKETS

Keep your pockets free of margarine.

GO TO WORK
ON YOUR DESK

Avoid keeping more than three
items on your desk that you
can't fit into your mouth.

WHAT'S UP DOC?

Never eat a meal in a room in which a
rabbit has recently died.

THE BENEFICIAL MUNIFICENCE OF FISH

A tank of lively guppies generates
energy and encourages get up and go.
However, if looking after fish
seems too much of a commitment,
positioning a kipper down the back of
a radiator will have the same effect.

ARE WE THERE YET?

If a road is less traveled
maybe it doesn't lead anywhere
particularly interesting.

OF ALL THE BARS

A wet bar of soap placed at the
top of a long flight of stairs is
bad Wrong Shui. Such bars are
more usefully positioned in the
bathroom in a secure soap dish.

ON REFLECTION

A mirror on the bedroom ceiling
reflects badly on you. Likewise
satin sheets, remote control lights,
and a baby oil dispenser on
the headboard.

Desks,
Ideal Location of

Do not place your desk anywhere
that you can get to it.

Or in the fast lane of the interstate.

CHANGING ROOMS

At all costs avoid letting anyone from
This Old House into your home.

SPREAD A LITTLE WARMTH

Fridges are, as a rule, cold,
unwelcoming places. Resolve the
problem by always leaving the
door slightly ajar.

WHERE?

When building large, expensive airports, it is best to locate them somewhere with easy access.

GO WITH THE FLOW, AGAIN

The rush of flowing water is also auspicious for the health of relationships.

If your relationship is in difficulty, try a skinny dip in the hot tub.

ON ROCKS AND HARD PLACES

Never position a rock
near a hard place.

THAT SINKING FEELING

This refers to that all-too-familiar
combination of impatience and
frustration encountered when
trying to find something in the
cupboard under the sink.

Eliminate the problem by fitting
your sink in the floor.

HARNESS THE MYSTICAL POWER OF CRYSTALS

A crystal hanging in a window will
focus good energy into your home.
Crystals hanging in front of the lenses
of your glasses will do the same
for your head.

DON'T LOOK BACK

Mirrors inappropriately positioned
can be very bad Wrong Shui.
They encourage you to look back on
the journey of life when you should
really be looking forward.

So remove all mirrors from your car.

DE-CLUTTER

A cluttered house allows bad Wrong Shui to accumulate in all its nooks and crannies. A simple and practical technique to reduce the negativity is to throw out everything belonging to your partner that he or she hasn't used or worn in the last month.

A LESSON FROM
THE MASTER

*It had been raining all day. No one had
stopped to buy flowers all afternoon.
Master Eu had spent much of the day
completing a 1:32 scale model of a Green-
Lipped New Zealand Mussel. Afterward I
watched as he took time out to butter the
inside of an empty Pringles tube. His
concentration would tolerate no
interruption. He was at one with his task.
And at one with the universe. I was*

contemplating what he had told me the day before. He had said, "Rhythm is a dancer."

It made no sense. But it made perfect sense.

That was the wonder of Master Eu.

And it was then that he summoned me to his side, shared an Aztec bar with me, and said with a slight radish in his voice,

"If we only get out of life what we put into it, why not just keep it in the first place and save a lot of wasted time and effort?"

How true.

BUILDINGS

It is well established that "walls
have ears" but lesser known that
"floors have noses" and totally
forgotten that "ceilings have elbows."

Act accordingly.

BAGUAS

In Wrong Shui the home is divided
into nine different bagua areas.
These link to your wealth, fame,
relationships, ancestors, health,
children, knowledge, career, and
benefactors. However, the most
important area is the "good school
district area." Make sure your home
is in one if you want your family
to prosper.

RIVER DEEP, MOUNTAIN HIGH

The ideal location for a house is with
a mountain behind it and water in
front. If your home lacks both, build
a pond directly outside your front door
and pile trash bags of rubbish
in your back garden until you've
built your own "mountain."

EGGSISTENTIALISM

Don't put all your eggs in one basket.

Use an egg carton like everyone else
and stop being such a poser.

THE JOURNEY TO ENLIGHTENMENT

In Wrong Shui life is seen as a cosmic journey, a struggle to overcome unseen and unexpected obstacles at the end of which the traveler will find illumination and enlightenment. Replicate this quest in your home by moving light switches away from doors and over to the far side of each room.

THE EDGE

It is far better to live close to the edge
than it is to have a copy of *Close to
the Edge* anywhere in your home.

THE FIVE ELEMENTS

Honor the five key elements:
fire, water, wind, earth, and ketchup.
Ignore any and your home will
not thrive. And especially pay heed
to the age-old Wrong Shui proverb, "A
house without ketchup is like the
Three Tenors without Pavarotti."

ARUMORTHERAPY

If your workplace lacks atmosphere,
position a different rumor
about your colleagues in each room.

CHIPPED PLATES

A chipped plate is
very bad Wrong Shui.

But a plate of chips is very good.

Directions for the Journey of Life

Always remember that in the journey
of life two wrongs don't make a right,
but three rights make a left.

LOVE IS

If your relationship is in trouble,
improve the situation by placing a
picture of an old partner with whom
you got on particularly well by your
bed. This should encourage
your current partner.

NIPPING THE PROBLEM IN THE BUD

If you are having trouble with
your neighbors, try to heal the rift
by planting a soothing hedge
of Japanese yews between
your properties.

WISDOM OF THE EAST

It is an indisputable fact that
wisdom from the East is far
wiser than wisdom from the West.
When speaking to a group of friends
or colleagues, stand on the east side of
the room and what you say will
be taken more seriously.

THE INCREDIBLE POWER
OF THE WISH LIST

If there is something you want
really badly, write it down on a piece
of paper 100 times. Do this every
day for 100 days. At the end of the
100 days you'll have completely
lost interest in what at one time
seemed your heart's desire.

BEAMS ARE BAD

Beams are exceedingly
bad Wrong Shui.

Steer clear of anyone who
beams at you, or comes
from California. They are
invariably untrustworthy.

COLUMNS ARE WORSE

Society has seen a proliferation of
totally useless newspaper and
magazine columns. They support
nothing but the egos and lifestyles
of the people who write them.
Your best policy is to ignore
them totally.

STAY GROUNDED

Earth is a powerful element in
Wrong Shui. Properly deployed it will
help ground you. If anyone at work is
getting carried away with their own
importance, spread soil over the
floor of their office and their desk.
The difference you notice in their
behavior will be remarkable.

THE SACRED GEOMETRY OF WRONG SHUI

There are circles to move in
and squares to avoid.

And a four-cornered triangle
is probably a pyramid.

Restaurant rules

In a restaurant never sit with
your back to the door.

But always sit with your
back to the bill.

SOME DAYS A HALF-DECENT BRAIN ISN'T QUITE ENOUGH

If you run a national sporting team,
positioning your foot in your mouth
could prove a severe disability.

A LESSON FROM THE MASTER

It had been raining all day, a fine, misty, slightly sarcastic rain that held within it the promise of doubt. In my time with Master Eu he had often remarked on weather and its influence on the chances of getting a cab on Oxford Street in rush hour.

Of course, what he was saying was really much more profound than that.

The secret was not just to listen, but to hear.

As dusk thickened I pored over the intricacies of a relatively large-scale dictionary trying to find the best way to get back to happiness. It was then that Master Eu leaned into the foam of my milk float, removed a log from my eye, and said,

"My friend, on any journey there is always a quicker route.

It's finding the route that takes time."

How true.

WHERE TO SIT

Never sit under a precariously
balanced heavy object.

LIGHTEN UP

Ladies, if you're having trouble
meeting men it may well be due to
inappropriate lighting in your homes.
Resolve the deficiency by placing a
red light bulb in the window of any
room facing the street.

THE ETIQUETTE
OF EATING

The kitchen and the dining area
should be as far away from each
other as possible. They should be at
least on different floors, preferably
in different houses, and ideally
in different ZIP codes.

THE DIVIDING RULE

Whenever entertaining friends for
dinner, avoid decorating the table with
tall candelabras, large flower
arrangements, or embalmed relatives
as they will divide the guests.

HOME SWEAT HOME

Condensation on windows is only
the atmosphere of your home
condensed into its liquid essence.
Collect it in Tupperware beakers
and sprinkle it anywhere you
want to feel more homely.

INTERIOR DESIGN

Always try to keep your lungs
positioned above your kidneys.

The Bells, the Bells

Doorbells resonate deeply through the
ether and give the listener pause for
thought and time to contemplate
universal harmony.

Encourage this by selecting a bell
that plays Beethoven's Fifth.

All of Beethoven's Fifth.

TAP THE POWER
OF TAPIOCA

A bowl of tepid tapioca strategically
located to the left of the front door
as you enter is mightily auspicious.
Especially if garnished with the navel
fluff of a retired IRS auditor.

It's surprising how much malice can fit behind a smile

In business, before any meeting begins, always check the room for hidden agendas.

THE PURIFYING POWER OF FIRE

In Wrong Shui fire is a living, vital force that, if used prudently, can purify a dwelling of negative energies. One simple technique to achieve this is to set fire to your curtains and stand back and watch as your home burns down. Any negative spirits will be driven away and the site will be pure.

IT'S WRITTEN IN THE STARS
(BEING A BRIEF INTRODUCTION TO WRONG SHUI ASTROLOGY)

In his travels around the globe Eu Plon Ka
navigated by the light and position of the
stars. While staring upward as he strode,
two revelations came to him. First he
realized, and I use his own words, "He who
walks with head in stars is easily tripped by
small protuberances." (How true.) Second,
he realized that the stars have arranged
themselves into certain eternal, easily

discernible shapes. Twelve shapes.
The twelve shapes, or signs, of the
Wrong Shui zodiac.

Now whereas Wrong Shui concerns itself
with placement in space, the Wrong Shui
zodiac concerns itself with placement in
time. In short, the year you were born
defines the person that you are.

What follows is but a small sip from the
vast lake that is the wisdom of Wrong Shui
astrology. To discover what it reveals
about you just check the year of your birth
against the relevant sign, then peruse
the following pages.

THE SHRUB 1900, 1912, 1924, 1936, 1948, 1960, 1972, 1984

THE COCKROACH 1901, 1913, 1925, 1937, 1949, 1961, 1973, 1985

THE MACAROON 1902, 1914, 1926, 1938, 1950, 1962, 1974, 1986

THE GROUT 1903, 1915, 1927, 1939, 1951, 1963, 1975, 1987

THE ARTICHOKE 1904, 1916, 1928, 1940, 1952, 1964, 1976, 1988

THE WINDBREAKER 1905, 1917, 1929, 1941, 1953, 1965, 1977, 1989

THE HALIBUT 1906, 1918, 1930, 1942, 1954, 1966, 1978, 1990

THE FLANGE 1907, 1919, 1931, 1943, 1955, 1967, 1979, 1991

THE MUMP 1908, 1920, 1932, 1944, 1956, 1968, 1980, 1992

THE MALIBU 1909, 1921, 1933, 1945, 1957, 1969, 1981, 1993

THE NIMBUS 1910, 1922, 1934, 1946, 1958, 1970, 1982, 1994

THE CUTLERY TRAY INSERT 1911, 1923, 1935, 1947, 1959, 1971, 1983, 1995

THE YEAR OF THE SHRUB

Shrubs are, for the most part, dull people. They are best suited to drab clothes and sheltered positions.

However, once a year, they will say or do something interesting. When they do they will want admiration and praise far in excess of what is deserved. But if all you can manage is an "Oooh, that's nice," don't worry. Shrubs will settle for this level of mild acknowledgment. Shrubs are reliable and they know their place.

THE YEAR OF THE COCKROACH

No one likes cockroaches. Even other cockroaches avoid the company of a cockroach. They are wriggly characters who scurry about scaring small children. They are also very good at spreading rumors. If gossip is a perennial problem at your workplace, find out if any of your colleagues are cockroaches and confront them with your suspicions.

Cockroaches should be watched carefully at all times. They should never be left alone with cake. The plus points of cockroaches are that they are good at hiding and will survive after a nuclear war.

THE YEAR OF THE MACAROON

On first meeting, macaroons seem lovely. They have a pleasingly solid exterior and a healthy complexion. However, when you get to know them better you will discover that they have a soft, malleable interior, and encounters with them leave a sweet, cloying taste in the mouth. For this reason macaroons seem to excel in all areas of PR.

It is worth noting that macaroons operate best in closed environments because if they are exposed to air or the harsh realities of the world for any length of time they go soggy. The Reform Party contains lots of macaroons.

THE YEAR OF THE GROUT

Grouts (or groutings as classic Wrong Shui traditionally describes them) are even more unappealing to look at than shrubs. They are the least exciting people you could hope to meet.

Having said that, the groutings
serve a vital purpose in society.
They help to stick things together.
They are the people who work
unobtrusively behind the scenes to
bind diverse humanity into a coherent
whole. For this reason grouts make
good interpreters, marriage guidance
counselors, and waiters.

THE YEAR OF THE ARTICHOKE

Artichokes are odd characters.
They don't fit in. They also tend to
worry the rest of the world. Not many
people know how to deal with them.
Not many people want to. For this
reason artichokes are often ignored.

However, if you can find a way
through an artichoke's spiky exterior,
you will find a surprisingly tender
heart. Eeyore was an artichoke.
Artichokes are scared of
melted butter.

THE YEAR OF THE WINDBREAKER

Windbreakers are very practical
people. They are also exceedingly
protective of their loved ones.
Windbreakers make excellent parents.
They are less desirable as lovers.
A windbreaker's idea of romance
will often be a long walk and
a packed lunch.

But if you find yourself rocked by the storms of life, a windbreaker makes an excellent companion. Windbreakers rarely amount to anything much in their chosen careers, but they can always be relied on to hand out a peppermint patty in a crisis.

THE YEAR OF THE HALIBUT

Halibuts are excitable, impetuous individuals. As such they totally lack judgment and perspective. Life for a halibut is just one long endless succession of opportunities. Halibuts should never be given any position of responsibility. You should even think twice about giving them positions of irresponsibility.

Despite this, every company should employ at least one halibut to balance out the doleful accumulated influence of shrubs and grouts. Never go into business with a halibut.

However, an affair would be interesting.

THE YEAR OF THE FLANGE

Flanges are very hard to describe.
They tend to be quite sloppy and
they very rarely persevere at anything.
In certain light conditions, around
dawn and dusk, they can disappear
completely. There is also something
indefinably sexual about everything
they do or say.

If you meet someone and have a
dubious feeling as to just how
appropriate the underwear
they're wearing is, chances are
that they are flanges.

Avoid them at all costs
at office parties.

THE YEAR OF THE MUMP

Among the main attributes of mumps
is the ability to engender mild
irritation in everyone they meet.
Mumps also tend to be quite childish
in their outlook. Mumps will insist,
when you go out for a meal in a
group, on only paying for precisely
what they've eaten. Mumps have few
friends. And the friends mumps do
have don't actually like them—they

just haven't got around to passing on the information. Mumps are also highly infectious. Spend any length of time in the company of a mump and by the next morning you, too, will be a mump. However, if you hung around with a mump as a child, you are probably immune to their mumpery.

THE YEAR OF THE MALIBU

Malibus are hopelessly unhip.
Unfortunately, in their own minds,
they are the very essence of the word
trendy. They even use the word trendy
to describe themselves in the personal
ads they are forever composing.
Malibus like to think of themselves as
the life and soul of the party. Even if
there isn't a party.
And if you finally convince them

that there isn't a party going on,
they'll only invite you to "the party
in my pants!!" (Malibus always use
exclamation marks when they speak.
Also when they think.) Most malibus
are men. Female malibus are scary
beyond words. Never let a malibu
start a conversation with a flange.

THE YEAR OF THE NIMBUS

Nimbi are large fluffy people with a large fluffy attitude about life. For them everything is a blue sky. They are welcoming and friendly and see good in everyone. For this reason nimbi are easily defrauded and are often passed over for promotion.

Nimbi are also very good at avoiding confrontations, floating away whenever they detect "something in the air." Indeed was it not the sublime Kate Adie who remarked to an admiring grocery store clerk that, "When the nimbi quit a country, I'm on the first plane out of there, baby."

THE YEAR OF THE CUTLERY TRAY INSERT

People born in the year of the cutlery tray insert tend to be very anal retentive. For them everything has a place, and everything should be in its place. Leave even a hair out of place in the environs of a cutlery tray insert and they'll be down on you like a ton of bricks. An exceedingly neatly stacked ton of bricks.

These people tend to be vociferous defenders of the status quo. They also actually keep gloves in the glove compartments of their cars. Never marry a cutlery tray insert. Your life will be intolerable. And any children you have will grow up to be serial killers.

SHELF SERVICE

Things on high shelves are
invariably hard to reach.

Position them on lower shelves
and you'll find them far
easier to get to.

THE UNSTABLE
TABLE OF LIFE

Tables with even-length legs are bad
Wrong Shui. They create a false sense
of security. It is far better to saw the
bottom off one leg. This will create an
irritating slope down which everything
you lay out for dinner slowly slides and
ends up in an awful mess in your lap.
This is a far better metaphor for the
futility of trying to organize your life.

A FITTING ENTRANCE

A door should never be bigger than
the space it has to fill.

CUT OUT KNIVES

Knives with sharp edges
are bad Wrong Shui.

In the kitchen only cut things with
spoons. Blunt spoons, ideally.

WHAT DO YOU THINK OF IT SO FAR?

Keeping all your rubbish in one
place increases negativity in the home.
It is far better to keep small piles of
rubbish in different
locations around each room
thus diminishing its potency.

TRUST

Where you place your trust is vitally
important. Try not to position it
anywhere that it can be manhandled or
purloined by ragamuffins
and buffoons.

Avoid being cornered

Rooms with angular corners will only
encourage you to be cornered in life.
Lessen the danger by stapling pickled
beets or meringues to the
apex of the corners.

WHAT'S YOUR VIEW?

The difference between curtains and blinds is a key to defining your view of the world. Those who favor curtains see the world as a movie. Those who favor blinds see the world as a lecture. Act accordingly.

A EUPHEMISM
FOR MANY THINGS

Never park a large car
in a small garage.

AUSPICIOUS ANIMALS

The pill bug, the garter snake,
and the daddy longlegs are all
considered excellent magnets
for good Wrong Shui.

Encourage them to visit your
home by advertising in
Better Homes and Gardens.

A LESSON FROM THE MASTER

It had been raining all day. I had just finished making a Ferrero Rocher-esque style pyramid out of pickled onions. The task had been set for me by The Master to get me to concentrate on, and contemplate, guilt.

Master Eu crouched in the corner of the milking shed silently walking through the dance moves from the latest Puff Daddy video. A pile of VAT returns lay undisturbed in a wok.

The Master summoned me to his side
with an enigmatic shimmer of his earlobe
and whispered,

"Gravy boats, gravy trains, why no
gravy planes?"

How true.

COLOR ME WONDERFUL

In Wrong Shui colors have meanings.
Red represents good fortune. Blue
stands for serenity. Green means
you should wash more frequently.
And gray is the new black.

IT'S IN THE GAPS BETWEEN WORDS THAT WE SAY THE MOST

In any conversation, the gaps between
the words the other person speaks
allow negative energies to slip through
and reach you. To avoid
this danger, fill these gaps
with low, atonal humming.

WHERE'S THE CHEESE?

Store food in your fridge
alphabetically.

HOW TO DE-CLUTTER YOUR HOME WITHOUT REALLY TRYING

Leave an open window when you go on vacation and when you return you'll find that the problems of a cluttered living space will have resolved themselves.

IT'S GOOD TO TALK

If a room feels cold and unwelcoming,
consider the fact
that you may have done
something to upset it.

Take it out for a nice, intimate
meal to discuss the matter.

A BRIEF MEDITATION ON THE INTRICACIES AND IRONIES OF THE ARCHITECTURE OF OFFICES

If you work in an office, always
remember that your floor
is someone else's ceiling.

But your ceiling is
someone else's floor.

NOT EVERYTHING SHOWS UP ON A SURVEY

Never buy a house with bloodstains on the wall and a strange smell coming from beneath the floorboards.

AN OLD WRONG SHUI PROVERB

There may be a shopping cart for
every pond, but there's not a pond
for every shopping cart.

TAKING THE CHILL OFF THE BED

If your marital relations lack
warmth, manipulate the comforter
so that it is all on your
side, not your partner's.

This should soon raise the temperature
in the bedroom.

WRONG SHUI
AND RETAILING

If lack of financial success has
hounded you through a succession of
failed business ventures, study of the
ancient principles of Wrong Shui
reveals that you can turn things around
by opening a shop selling
old rope and hot cakes.

CARPETS

Avoid walking on carpets.

How shelvish

On shelves, position books with spines
facing inward.

This way reading becomes a true
search for enlightenment.

THE DESERT AT NIGHT— THE WELL IN THE DESERT

If you get thirsty in the
night, position a glass of
water by your bedside.

The problem will soon disappear.

WHO PUT THAT THERE?

When driving, avoid roads
with forks in them.

In fact, avoid roads with
any silverware in them.

THAT SINKING FEELING, AGAIN

Place used tea bags in the sink to
encourage conversation in the home.

BEHIND YOU

Always keep your back passage
free of obstructions.

"HELLO, I'VE JUST MOVED IN"

When moving into a new home, an old
fridge or washing machine
positioned carefully by the walk to
your front door will help you to
meet your neighbors.

THE CRAMMED CLOSET

A crammed closet clutters up your
energy field at the start of the day.
Solve the problem by strewing clean
and dirty clothes all around the place.
You'll be surprised by how quickly the
"crammed closet" problem disappears.

A LESSON FROM THE MASTER

It had been raining all day. The Master paused from scraping the mildew off the Scotch egg he had been mentoring all summer.

"In many ways," he said, "a man's life is like a shoe."

"The heel is your past. The sole is your future. And the laces are the present that bind your past and future together."

I contemplated this wisdom as I watched
The Master rub Ben-Gay into a turnip.

And a query fluttered into my mind like a
butterfly alighting on a Mars Bar.

"Master?" I ventured, "what about slip-ons?"

Without hesitation The Master kneed me in
the groin and said,

"No one likes a smart ass."

How true.

How very, very true.

ANOTHER OLD
WRONG SHUI PROVERB

Foolish are the people who play

Twister on the stairs.

WHICH WAY DOES YOURS SWING?

Doors to a bedroom should
only open one way.

Doors that swing both ways
can easily be misinterpreted.

YOU ONLY HAVE TO ASK

Activate the wealth corner of any crowded room by standing in it with a large kitchen knife and a sign that reads GIVE ME ALL YOUR MONEY.

SITTING PRETTY

To reduce anxiety and annoyance in
your home, position toilet paper rolls
where they can easily be reached from
a sitting position on the toilet.

TABLES AND CHAIRS

Never put tables and chairs
in the same room.

If they congregate together
for any length of time,
they will inevitably hatch plots
against you and your pets.

YET ANOTHER OLD WRONG SHUI PROVERB

(YES, I KNOW, THERE ARE A LOT OF THEM)

To break a glass ceiling
you need a hard head.

SLEEPING PARTNERS

Never start a relationship
with a new partner on a mattress
that an old partner is still sleeping on.

THE UNIVERSAL CYCLE

To signal your spiritual oneness with
the universal cycle of life, never go
out without wearing bicycle clips.

THE POWER
OF SPAGHETTI

Spaghetti (or stick pasta) when
stored in contact with itself acts as
a magnet for bad Wrong Shui. If you
must keep spaghetti in the house,
weaken its negative power by
wrapping each strand in cling wrap
before storage.

NEGATIVE AURAS, THE CLEANSING OF

If a man in a bar is annoying you
with unpleasant behavior, cleanse
his aura and calm him down by
hopping around him on one foot
three times and chanting the name
of The Master—Eu Plon Ka—
while pointing at him with the sacred
Wrong Shui gesture of the fist with
extended middle finger.

HOW TO IMPROVE
YOUR LIFE OUT OF
ALL RECOGNITION

Small books, abundantly scattered
throughout the home and workplace
and liberally dispensed to friends and
acquaintances create excellent Wrong
Shui for you for 101 years and 101
days. Particularly potent are *The Little
Book of Wrong Shui*, *The Little Book
of Stress*, and the Christmas classic
The Stocking Filler.